Beneath the Tall Black Door

Four Seasons on River Street

Nature parables for righting
our everyday affairs

Jacqueline K. Kelsey, Ph.D.

AuthorHouse™
1663 Liberty Drive
Bloomington, IN 47403
www.authorhouse.com
Phone: 1-800-839-8640

© 2011 Jacqueline K. Kelsey, Ph.D. All rights reserved.

No part of this book may be reproduced, stored in a retrieval system, or transmitted by any means without the written permission of the author.

First published by AuthorHouse 3/2/2011

ISBN: 978-1-4520-7039-1 (hc)
ISBN: 978-1-4520-7040-7 (sc)
ISBN: 978-1-4520-7041-4 (e)

Library of Congress Control Number: 2010914831

Printed in the United States of America

This book is printed on acid-free paper.

Because of the dynamic nature of the Internet, any Web addresses or links contained in this book may have changed since publication and may no longer be valid. The views expressed in this work are solely those of the author and do not necessarily reflect the views of the publisher, and the publisher hereby disclaims any responsibility for them.

ABOUT THE AUTHOR'S RELATIONSHIP TO NATURE

By telling parables Jacqueline Kelsey teaches observational skills regarding the connection between revered nature and the commonplace of human experience.

After completing interdisciplinary Ph. D. research on learning from the land, Jacqueline developed a theoretical worldview which illustrates how imagination relates to cycles in nature, work life, and learning.

Her professional background as a college and university teacher has been enhanced by extensive travel throughout the United States and beyond. Her exploration has included immersion in native cultures which are historically embedded in the wonder of nature such as the American Indian, Hawaiian and South Pacific. Growing up in a rural community provided her with first-hand experience nurturing animals. She is able to draw naturally on true-to-life incidents occurring on their once-family farm and in small towns where she lived throughout her life.

Dedicated to learning how untamed nature can bring meaning and healing through its all encompassing beauty, Kelsey has used her accumulated talents to share what she has learned through serendipity and intuition.

Through the spoken word on radio programs and in workshops, and through the written word in books and materials, she conveys a simple method of seeing and hearing. Nature deserves an integral role in developing our awareness. She has come to believe that tuning into our imagination makes us one with a God-imagined natural world and therefore enlarges our significance on earth.

PREFACE

Learn to hear and see your answers from nature. On the front porch of Kathryn and John's North Woods' home along the river, seven stories join the worlds of home and wild nature beneath the tall black door. Together the stories illustrate the healing touch of nature in our affairs when we learn to imagine life as children do. Story events transform into everyday miracles which guide the main characters' lives.

John and Kathryn draw nature to themselves to learn about finding joy in grief, balancing overwork with leisure, saying "No" to negative influences, having faith to heal, and confirming intuitive leads for career changes. Readers can recognize their connections with nature and become inspired by example to right their affairs when they pay attention to their hearts' desires for improving their lives.

Intuitive observations and sensitivity to nature's creatures enable the author's main characters to teach us a way of thinking and behaving that successfully translates everyday, backyard experiences into nurturing food for the soul.

Beneath the Tall Black Door represents a portal for those who choose to respectfully allow nature to reveal connections and solutions to the issues they currently face.

With elegant simplicity the parables contained in *Beneath the Tall Black Door* become a guide to discover a deeper appreciation for the profound messages that nature reveals through its cycles.

The author's imaginative description of the four changing seasons on River Street clearly gives the reader a philosophical sense of the majestic beauty of the wild and what it has to offer us.

DEDICATION

"Nellie with the Big Eyes"

Miss Nellie viewed the river from her pinnacle banister inside the house on River Street.

Nellie (NOEL) was found under a snowy porch in December. The neighbor who loved animals gave her to John even though he did not want a dog or a rabbit. Nellie had become the youngest cat in the house because Thomas Aquinas, the "Venerable old Tom," had flown from the farm to the North Woods to spend his last days sunning in the window of the birthing room. He would descend the steep steps one at a time like a small child and Nellie would bounce over him skipping steps.

When Kathryn moved back to the Midwestern farm, Kathryn helped her parents in their last years and took

Nellie with her after Tom died. When Nellie died suddenly from an enlarged heart, she left behind friends-- Blackie and Keyesport who grieved mightily for days. Her "Garden Girl" headstone statue poses like she did for her picture to be taken in front of every holiday decoration.

APPRECIATION

Family influence and tutelage have created the stories which enact beneath the tall black door on River Street.

Hans lived in the house and experienced the animals; so therefore, he took interest in recalling the incidents as he edited. Jamie, a librarian at Greenville College (my alma mater) in Illinois, edited and prepared the text and pictures for publication. Her bright, quick-minded responses to content concerns were invaluably supportive. Robin, of Vermont, a graphic designer and marketing specialist, came into my life again after fifteen years when she had created a promotional pamphlet for my workshops and writings. Her flare for synthesizing ideas created the author information and book promotions.

Thirty-years or more of influences have prepared me for seeing and hearing and creating my heart's desires in story. My parents' farm home provided the setting for many natural experiences in the fields and woods and with animals. Folklore professor, Larry Danielson, University of Illinois, led me through farm traditions in folklore and inspired me to see and hear life with its common life aesthetics.

Finally, little Grandma Kelsey's example of successfully caring for small creatures provided the example of attending to the needs of animals. My father loved to tell the story of her taping a popsicle stick to a broken bird's wing. Family stories preserving similar healings tell how Mother nursed the wound of our horse that jumped the barbed wire fence and Dad's cleaning out the festering belly of a baby raccoon which had been gored.

The desire of my heart to see and hear and heal and be healed accumulates in life story so that I gratefully live my life with awareness of the natural world, which surrounds, supports, and inspires us all to live in connection with community and God.

Jacqueline Kelsey

PARABLES

Evening Song   —   1

"May I Come In?" said the Sparrow   —   13

The Miracle Moose   —   31

Memorial Day Mouse   —   43

Dance Above the Flowers   —   53

The Wild Cat   —   69

The Dancing Rabbit   —   87

Create Your Parables   —   111

Open My Eyes that I May See

-- An old hymn

EVENING SONG

"She noticed the green words printed on the paper towel—Health and Happiness. Her only assist, she spoke the words as if they were a benediction."

Jacqueline K. Kelsey, Ph.D.

Kathryn and John ordinarily would build a fire in the wood stove and eat soup and sandwiches on T. V. trays in front of the living room fire. Tonight, they sat at the kitchen table for supper. Outside, the evening was warm, like summer leaves floating down among the dried flower stalks. The tall black wooden door propped open to cool off the house; the glass storm door had been put in for the winter.

Kathryn had to drive twelve miles to arrive at song practice by 6:30; it was already 6:00 o'clock. She shot up from the table at 6:20 knowing it was too late. The drive through the country took twenty minutes to arrive at the rural village where the group practiced in the community building. Running through the dining room, she grabbed her sweater off the door peg because the air would cool down after practice. Fall evenings in the North Woods were chilly.

She pushed herself through the front storm door sideways and stepped hard onto the blue front porch carpet. The yellow bug light created an eerie fall night. Her knees locked when she stopped herself abruptly. She could not take another step. On the blue carpet **beneath the tall black door** lay a taupe-colored bird the size of a model airplane—tilted back on its side, with its wing straight up; it had crash-landed. Its long beak pointed straight up. The wide-open eye stared, trance-like.

She stared at its chest to see if it breathed. "Was it alive?" Kathryn wondered. Gently, in and out, the soft feathers lay easily on its speckled breast. In and out, in and out, the soft feathers gave way to its automatic breathing. John was at the kitchen table. Kathryn raced into the kitchen to forewarn him. He said he had heard the sound of it hitting the glass.

Out the kitchen door to the woodshed, she searched for a container, shoe box size, and sent John in to the side yard to grab handsful of leaves to fill the box. "Hurry," she called, while she tore off a paper towel on the kitchen counter and urged John to the front porch with her. The upstairs hall light filled the narrow staircase passage behind them and glowed against the storm door glass.

Kathryn instructed John to fill the shoebox with leaves. She could not touch the bird. Feeling the wild life in her hand was too intimate. Perhaps it was the fear of feeling death in her hand that made her dig her elbows into her ribs. "NO." She gestured no with her hands.

John did not seem to mind. The paper towel would create a barrier to the life or death inside. The bird felt John's hand closing around it. When John set the bird on the blue rug, the bird shifted its head upright. Its beak pointed forward. Kathryn could see that the bird looked alert, like always. Still holding lightly, John moved his arm, crane-like, from the middle of the blue carpet toward the shoebox pushed up against the balustrade to steady it. As he lowered his stiff crane arm, Kathryn noticed that the towel would be under the bird's feet and a larger corner would be left over. She wanted to cover the bird so it would feel secure. The half-opened eyelids shut out the light and the pain. Kathryn reverently knelt next to the shoe box. Quietly, she watched the motionless bird. It looked severely injured--no longer dazed, but rather overcome by the pain holding it still.

Kathryn knew that she was only human help; she had called on all her childhood know-how. "Shoe boxes were good for most houses—cards for school chums on Valentine's Day, miniature doll houses, dioramas, and burial chambers." Supper had been rushed, and the bird was dying. She was already late for singing practice. Leaning against the balustrade, her mind whispered, "How can I leave the bird?" The patient bird had accepted the shoebox and even the paper towel. What could she do?

She noticed the green words printed on the paper towel-- HEALTH AND HAPPINESS. Her only assist, she spoke the words like they were a benediction, not knowing what good they would do. Would her words heal a bird? Kathryn felt better when she could do something that she **knew** would help. She knew it would not help to sit with the bird and felt that she had to keep her commitment to herself to sing.

When she arrived at the basement of the community building, the group stopped singing to welcome Kathryn. She explained that a bird had flown into the storm door and she took time to nest it in a box with leaves and a paper towel over it. When she recounted the "health and happiness" message the ladies smiled sympathetically while they tilted their heads knowingly. What did they know? After the harmony began she forgot about the bird. She would not have to face knowing about the bird's fate until she climbed the porch steps leading to the tall black door.

On the drive home she felt calm. John, too, had gone to a choir rehearsal. She knew song lifts. It was magical when she felt lighter after singing with the ladies. She wondered about how John felt singing in the bass section. He, too, would have to face knowing about the injured bird.

Before leaving John had shut the wooden door so that no light from the hall would shine through the storm door. No other birds would fly into the see -through glass; the porch was dark.

Kathryn stood for a moment on the top step. She dreaded lifting the paper towel to see whether or not the bird would be dead or would have flown away. From the steps she could see the "HEALTH AND HAPPINESS" towel was half over the damp leaves. Kathryn knelt down next to the balustrade as if she were in prayer. Carefully, lifting the damp corner tip of the towel, she saw that the bird had moved; white and gray droppings dotted the white paper. The bird must have heard her song; it had refueled and lifted. It was well enough to take off—to fly away—a miracle in her spirit.

When John came home at 8:00 o'clock she met him at the gate. "How was song practice?" John asked. How could he not remember to ask about the bird first of all? Perhaps he had avoided thinking about the bird. She was angry and kept a solemn face. "You'll have to look for yourself," she spurted out. He too saw dark droppings on the white towel. John was silent for a moment. When he lifted the towel he exclaimed, "How was song practice?" Kathryn hummed, "I told the women about the bird."

Kathryn and John shivered on the top step while mulling over the bird's take-off. The cold night air banked around the porch. "How was your rehearsal?" asked Kathryn, wondering if he would give a clue to his feelings. "Wonderful. The bass section always lifts the sopranos for flight. We support the whole choir." Kathryn knew he felt important. Perhaps he would realize that he, too, helped the bird to fly away.

A child's innocent vision of the present allows reality to bend to the desires of the child's heart. What appears as unusual is usual.

"MAY I COME IN?" SAID THE SPARROW

She thought, I cannot stand in the bay window until the dark hides us both!

Jacqueline K. Kelsey, Ph.D.

Kathryn watched the sparrow up close, with her full body next to the window where the bird pecked at the seeds on the bird tray. "She must see me—my shadow?" Kathryn said to herself as she stood motionless, listening to her own breathing while the bird stayed to peck. Balancing on its toothpick legs, the bird barely bobbed its head when it pecked at the snow-covered seeds on the bird tray, which was nailed to the porch railing outside the bay window.

Even though the morning sun was out, the bird puffed up its feathers to keep warm. Kathryn worried that later it would be cold in the winter wind after sundown. She looked beyond the bird feeder tray and saw a cave-like bush. "The bird could fly under the boughs to stay warm," she speculated.

The boughs of the Bridal Wreath bush had bent to the ground under the weight of the snow cap heaped on its crown. Under the boughs of snow the sparrow would have a perfectly warm cave. She thought, of course, that the space was too large for such a tiny body; even so, she felt relief.

While Kathryn continued to watch the puffed-up bird through the window, she felt that her own body had become a gentle shield for it, almost like a cave. She wanted to protect the quiet, small bird. "What should I do next?" she wondered. "I cannot stand in the window until darkness hides us both! I'll make a house over the bird feeder tray!" Then she remembered that mother birds are scared away from their nests and that they do not return to their eggs if you touch the nest and leave your human scent. Would she scare away the bird? She decided to wait until John came home after school at three o'clock.

In the afternoon, Kathryn watched and waited from inside the bay window. The sparrow had flown away during the morning. "Would the sparrow return to the feeder at the end of the day?" she asked herself. "Where was it now?" she wondered. The other birds had not come either and the feeding time was over. She hoped that the sick bird would huddle with the others where they knew how to keep warm, in a place like the Bridal Wreath cave. But then Kathryn questioned whether or not the other birds would let the sick bird in. While all the other birds had eaten together on the feeding tray, the sick bird had pecked by herself at the opposite end of the tray; obviously the other birds were staying away from her.

When John came home at three o'clock, the bird had not returned yet. The two stood in the bay window waiting, feeling disappointed and helpless. Earlier that morning John had commented that the bird's movements had slowed down to the speed of a slow motion film. Finally, while they waited in vain for the bird to return for food, they began to fear that the bird might be sicker than it was in the morning. "Maybe she would never return," they thought.

At that moment Kathryn made her decision and told John about it. Hastily, she hurried to the woodshed on the opposite end of the house. She found a shallow, rectangular box propped against the garbage can. The box, formerly full of soup cans, was an extra one John had been saving to collect black twigs and tree bark which blew off the trees in late fall and winter.

On her kitchen table, she covered the soup can box with two long sheets of wax paper, one for the length and one for the width of the box, and carefully taped the paper over the outside to keep the box dry. Carrying the transposed soup can box, she glided over the smooth wooden floors of the dining room, through the front door, and onto the slippery slanted porch. She stepped carefully over to the side porch railing and fitted the box under the tray and around the open sides of the feeder tray so the wind would not blow on the wobbly bird when it pecked at the seeds. When she had finished, she brushed the snow off her skirt and shivered back to the kitchen.

Outside the winter evening wrapped around the warm house like a fluffy, white rabbit stole. The fire popped inside the Alpiner woodstove in the living room. Their mystical cat, Thomas Aquinas, nestled in the corner of the sofa on his Icelandic wool blanket, folded in layers to make it extra soft to comfort his arthritis.

In the kitchen, Kathryn and John washed the supper dishes. She kept thinking about the birds and the feeder while she dipped her dishes in and out of the warm, soapy water. After rinsing the last cup she hurried out through **the tall black door,** onto the dusty white porch. Enough snow had blown onto the floor that she slowly pressed one moccasin into the snow at a time to keep from slipping on the slick, painted boards. Shaking each foot, getting her ankles wet, she made her way to the balustrade railing outside the bay window.

Disappointingly, the birds had not returned to the feeder as Kathryn hoped they would. Powder flakes had begun to form a frozen glaze over the bumpy seeds on the bird feeder tray; it looked like the top of a sheet cake covered with vanilla icing poured over tiny nut pieces.

She would make it possible for the birds to eat even though the prospect of their return seemed improbable.

Breaking the crust, she sifted the snow from the sunflower seeds and then rubbed her red fingers together as if they were matchsticks, hoping for a spark. When she had fully uncovered the seeds she again padded in her moccasins toward the door. Footprints, twice as big as her own, followed her like monster shoes back to **the tall black door**.

Looking back she swayed with the leafless tree limbs floating in the wind like black skeletons dressed in white shirts. This was the kind of gray cold that made John and her want to spend the evening by the woodstove.

At 11:00 they reluctantly closed the heavy, black iron doors of their wood stove full of glowing embers, and creaked up the fifteen steep steps of their old 1820 house. The cold brittle planks of their bedroom floor sang loudly.

Under heavy layers of blankets, Kathryn thought about the small creatures knowing how to find the best places for themselves. Although she had hope, she also worried that the bird was too sick to live. Conflict between hope and worry worsened and she rolled from one side to the other in order to get more comfortable. Feeling helpless because she could not see how anything had been accomplished by fixing up the soup can shelter, she finally asked herself if praying for the bird could help. But then she thought that the bird was too small for her to pray over and have her prayer answered. She wondered if God would care about her desire for the bird to get well. She sighed and pulled her knees to her chest to make a ball so she could rock herself to sleep.

When she awakened, dawn had begun to push up its light into the dark gray horizon. Soon she would see a familiar pink backdrop behind the mountains as the sun rose higher. She could feel her breath streaming into the cold air layer above her wool blankets. It was time to get up and she knew how to stretch her legs straight over the side

Beneath the Tall Black Door

of the bed in order to find her slippers and avoid stepping on the cold pine boards with her bare feet.

After breakfast John and Kathryn stood watching near the bay window in the living room. It was too early for the birds to be feeding; they usually came when it was fully light. The two sat quietly on the French high back sofa next to the bay window. Finishing their coffee, they waited to see if their sparrow would return to the feeder by herself. "Would she be sick?" they wondered.

It was 7:30—time to go to school—and no birds had come to feed. Snow had piled up blanket-deep in the night. The two bundled up in fleece scarves, rabbit fur-lined mittens and earmuffs, and felt-lined tall leather boots. Feeling prepared for the cold, Kathryn opened **the tall black door** onto their front porch surrounded with the graceful balustrade. Ah! She breathed swirls of soft crystals into the cold air column around her.

In the bright light of morning the icy tree figurines looked like dancers frozen on stage. The snow peaked

six inches high on the proscenium-like railing wrapped around the porch. John and Kathryn entered the winter stage. They sensed the awe of the morning white snow scene and made their debut onto the royal blue carpet runner leading from the tall black door to the steps. They stepped out to take a bow to morning. Suddenly both of them stiffened, like they had heard someone calling out FREEZE in the childhood game.

In the middle of the royal blue carpet, plumped down on her toothpick legs, the tiny wound-down bird presented herself to them in the pale yellow morning light. Wide-eyed, she blinked her shiny bee-bee eyes. Tilting her head from side to side, she seemed to listen patiently, or at least unafraid, while they watched and talked about her. The bird remained still, changing her weight from foot to foot.

John and Kathryn leaned closer, within two feet. "She has returned to us," Kathryn softly exclaimed. John's soft eyes spoke to Kathryn: "She has returned to show us that we made a difference—she is well." Kathryn believed her desire for the bird to get well had been enough—even though she did not have much faith—not enough faith to ask for what she wanted. At that moment, John and Kathryn felt as close to the sparrow as if she were their puppy.

The bird looked strong. Her neck and head were upright instead of being drawn into her body. She stretched her toothpick legs tall so that her body looked like a large egg set on top of a pair of stilts. How tiny she was compared to the long blue carpet, the tall black door, and their large bodies. But John and Kathryn felt that literal size made no difference and that they were sharing equal space in the huge proportions of human dimensions and the outdoors.

Kathryn felt the same closeness as she did yesterday when she became the sparrow's cave-shield through the window glass, but today she and the sparrow were together without a glass barrier between them. "Does the bird realize how close we are?" she asked John.

Amazed, John said, "She wants to come in." It seemed to him that she was waiting to be asked. She did not hop aside or fly away. John uttered a possibility so convincing that Kathryn said loudly inside herself, "No!" because she was afraid. She remembered that while they were on vacation a huge black bird had fallen down their chimney and flown around the house until it wearied and died. "She cannot come in," Kathryn protested firmly to John.

As she spoke, the sparrow raised itself up gracefully from the carpet. "Has she completed a mission to show me that desire does make a difference?" Kathryn wondered and her heart quieted after the sparrow disappeared over the wood shed.

Turning back to John she noticed the cylinders of Birch bark near the tall black door. Last Saturday she had gathered them on her walk, a mile up Forest Hill Road into the woods, behind their house. She had left them on the porch because the next day she had intended to create a woodland décor under the bay window. Kathryn asked herself, "Had the sparrow slept all night in the Birch bark?" She wondered whether or not she had provided for the bird. Had the sparrow chosen the cylinder for its natural housing? Had they matched their desires? Maybe it was possible to be on the same wave-length with nature? These thoughts crowded her mind.

They waited on the top steps perplexed about the bird looking at them for so long, standing so close to them. "Did the sparrow return to reassure us?" John asked her. "Obviously, it was well!" he said. Before Kathryn came down the steps, John shuffled the snow off the steps with his big leather boots; he looked up at her and smiled. "You may have kept the sparrow from flying into the house when she asked to come in, but her return will be with us always," he said.

At the end of the sidewalk Kathryn pulled and pushed at the picket fence gate to make a path through. The snow wedged behind the gate. When she looked back she saw on their path the shape of an angel's wing, like the kind you make when you lie down in the snow and press and flap your arms and legs hard into the snow.

The thought of childhood play brought to her mind a childhood-learned Bible verse about God caring for people in small ways—He cared enough to number the hairs on their heads just like He gave safety to the sparrows. Her heart warmed at the thought. Doubt about praying for small things was gone. John walked through the gate behind her. Cupping her hands she directed a hushed voice toward the river. "The sparrow is our winter angel."

All is well with my soul. -- An old hymn

THE MIRACLE MOOSE

"...her entire body bellowed a 'NO' which sounded like an animal's voice—breathy, gray-deep and guttural."

Jacqueline K. Kelsey, Ph.D.

There is a myth along the Moose River in the North Woods. Out of the woods each year a moose trots down the blacktop, dead-end street in front of Kathryn and John's home. He comes to announce spring. Last year, the neighbor who worked at the hardware store reported seeing the moose come out of the woods onto the blacktop.

Kathryn had not yet seen a moose in the North Woods. Many times she would mistake a log in the river for a floating moose. Often she would scan the edges of the woods where fields spilled out. How could she feel part of the New England culture when she had never seen a moose? Giving up, she bought a china moose that she could see through the glass door of their built-in dining room cupboard.

Stories circulate frequently about how dangerous a moose can be when it collides with a car. Recently Kathryn heard the friends of a fatal victim report that the moose's head shoved through the windshield. By contrast, Kathryn's image painted an almost pre-historic moose. She imagined a moose of grandeur, under the spell of the full moon, tossing his gigantic antlers and pawing the turf of a pine grove, glistening in the mist of a late autumn night.

On Sunday morning Kathryn drove with John to a town twenty miles away for Sunday brunch. For several weeks they had been discussing summer plans, visits, and visitors. This morning John announced that he would say yes to his friend's summer visit for a week.

Kathryn was furious because she had said no several times. The visit would mean spending their week's vacation with the guest and paying for overnights as they traveled. The alternative was taking day trips and entertaining him in their home which she did not want to do. Kathryn had made her arguments. The friend was not a mutual one; in fact, she did not like his drinking and his negative philosophy of life. Kathryn and John argued many times over the issue. She had said no in many ways—polite and persuasive, and also with hurt and anger. It seemed as if she were practicing saying no—a rehearsal, perhaps.

Several miles out of town the woods ended; small crop fields checkered the landscape. Across from the longest section of field, the huge regional power plant towered over the fields from the right side of the road. As they drove, John and Kathryn resumed "the visit" discussion once again on their way north for Sunday brunch.

They had been battling for three days. Kathryn felt anxious not knowing when the friend would call back and what John would say; they could not come to a firm, agreeable decision. Without her consent, several years before, they had visited the friend in New Mexico; she feared the pain of being disregarded. During arguments, money and time were major factors but most of all, she was uncomfortable with the friend's drinking pattern when they spent time together. Feeling unimportant to John brought on her depression.

For the thousandth time she had said **no,** but this time, riding in the car, across from the power plant, John said, "He is coming," as if he had no control over the situation. She turned sideways toward the driver's seat and window. Standing on her knees in the car seat, she faced him. With her entire body Kathryn released a breathy, guttural, and gray-deep "**NO**."

She listened to her voice, a powerful wild animal's bellow, like the buck she heard late last fall. Walking the field-row next to the woods she had surprised the buck just before he leaped into the woods. Both waited still, looking at each other. The buck gusted a life-cry she felt before it arched over the fence. Never had she yelled a life-cry like life in the wild. She, too, had pushed her total life energy into her surviving voice just as she and John drove by the power plant towering above the field. She glanced through the rear view mirror on John's side, quickly panning the scene behind the car. The setting had passed—the woods, the field, and the power plant. The mirror zoomed in and framed the witness.

At the edge of the field posed an elegant, statuesque moose cow. In a freeze-frame Kathryn could see the bony features of her slim head and her delicate soft face and ears. She had not expected such grace and finesse in the statuary of a moose! "John, John, see her?" He glanced, but not in time before she disappeared into the woods. It seemed she had appeared out of nowhere. Had she been crossing the field on a triangle from the east to the south as they also moved? Kathryn wondered about pre-knowledge. Did her thought and need precede the appearance so they were simultaneous? She had not seen her cross the wide triangle. She was a real mythical creature.

At the moment, Kathryn was the strongest in her life. In a place of true North, the moose cow had appeared for her to see. The moose was Kathryn's witness. As she rode north in calm, Kathryn reminded herself of reading a Native American belief that the moose bull becomes its most assertive self in seclusion. Kathryn had needed male assertiveness. She had been living in seclusion for several years, in the Northwest, gathering herself toward a true life, the one she could picture now.

Curiously, the friend's call never came. Kathryn believed that her force, her spoken word, had displaced all other energy to end the intrusion, which was energy unlike herself. She had been heard. She had gusted the silent NO she had been screaming all of her life.

In the next few weeks John continued to quiz Kathryn about the mystery of his friend coming to visit. He had not called to confirm or cancel the visit. John wondered if Kathryn had betrayed him and called the friend to tell him no. It was unlike his friend not to call. Kathryn wondered if "the friend" had heard her refusal.

Most of all, Kathryn had called out and been heard by the moose she desired to see—her own assertive, surviving self. The "Spring Myth" would re-enact on the

Jacqueline K. Kelsey, Ph.D.

blacktop street and in the home where she and John lived. John was relieved that he did not have to choose between his friend and Kathryn. Probably he would not create another situation like this one. John could report a new story about moving encounters with moose.

What a child seeks, he finds. -- An old verse

MEMORIAL DAY MOUSE

"A tiny ball, the size of her thumb, seemed to be racing with her."

The weeds luxuriated in the side yard. Weed killer would not solve the problem because John and Kathryn wanted to protect Elizabeth. She had dug her tunnel next to the roundel garden. Kathryn and John were willing to pull weeds by hand until they got them all. The year before, John had worked to pull all the Creeping Charlie behind the garage. This spring the grass had thickened and there was hardly any Charlie.

Kathryn had not trimmed before the snowfall. The bushes needed trimming and the roundel and perennial flower borders alongside the barn needed clearing out from last fall. Sometimes she left tall weeds for the birds to light on and use for crafting their nests. It seemed like all the pulling, trimming, and clearing needed to be done on Memorial Day if the yard was to make a show of readiness for early summer flowers. All the tools—rake, hoe, trowel, shears—lay next to the roundel. Kathryn was hauling the refuse across the road to throw it over the riverbank. The tall riverbank cane had already grown half its height.

After working all morning, she felt weak. Where was the Memorial Day fun? She and John had not planned a picnic or cookout like their neighbors down the street. John and Kathryn were new in town. They would use the time off from school to work. Kathryn thrived on yard work—cleaning up refuse, planting, cutting flowers. She considered it therapy. Actually, she loved working hard for its own sake; it was a challenge to trim big bushes and haul refuse to throw over the riverbank.

Nearly noon, it was getting hot. She was sweating and needed a break when her neighbor, Karen, walked by on the outside of the picket fence. Because of the tall, bright blooming Forsythia bushes they could hardly see each other. Karen yelled, "Are you having a good Memorial Day?" Kathryn fanned herself with her hat and shouted flippantly, "I am going to work myself to death." When she heard herself she knew it was testy to use those words.

Who heard her pun on celebrating the Memorial Day? The new neighbor sauntered home retorting, "I guess you are going to work…."

Kathryn returned to the watering can. Wanting recognition for her work, she had asked for it in a negative way. How thoughtless! As she bent over to pick up her trowel, she could see that a small mouse had been squashed near her newly planted Pansies. It was not there when she started planting. Calling to John, she stared at the tiny creature. "Come quickly; look in the Pansies."

Waiting for him, she knew that she had spoken the words of death and told John the prediction that had come true. She had taunted in jest—but death to herself, not the mouse. Angling through the back fence gate next to the barn, John carried the squashed mouse on her trowel. He carefully wedged it between Day Lily spears while she shuffled across the tar road. Her feet and legs felt heavy. She was tired from working; her feet were hot and swollen.

All of a sudden, a marble-size, fat bug rolled in front of her too-tight canvas garden shoes. A tiny ball the size of her thumb seemed to be racing with her. She followed it to the gate, next to the barn. When it rolled as far as the Rose trellis in the flower border next to the barn, there was nowhere for it to roll except over a large rock. How could it? Kathryn wanted to help. When she leaned down closely with the trowel she could see ears. It looked like a baby mouse. Scooping the trowel under it she tried to provide a platform to help it crawl over the rock. To a tiny mouse the rock was as large as the mountain rising straight up behind her rock garden outside the kitchen window.

The mouse was slippery; it moved so fast that the back of the trowel skipped on the sidewalk. The baby's eyes were closed; in fact, it was so small you could hardly tell its body from its head. There was a crack between the barn and the rock and the mouse scooted along the bottom of the rock disappearing into the Hosta border. Kathryn knew that the mouse would not find its mother near the roundel. It seemed that was where the baby was headed. She wondered if it was old enough to live.

John and Kathryn sat in Adirondack chairs and talked over the day's plans. Certainly they could take a nap. Maybe drive over to a state park. With a spark of energy in his voice John suggested a sack lunch and a walk up the mountain behind the house. What a memorable day to celebrate living life more easily. She would take her neighbor, Karen, a Pansy bouquet late in the afternoon so the flowers would not wilt. After all, she did believe in life—especially for small creatures. She would always remember her "chase after life."

When you have lost your way,

discover your heart's desire and

experience oneness with God.

DANCE ABOVE

THE FLOWERS

"The bird danced in one place without taking a sip of nectar. In fact, Kathryn had never seen her sip nectar from any of the flowers."

Kathryn relished the warmth of this last week of August, almost the end of summer. She sunned herself on the front porch where she typed her manuscript at a small, round, glass table, topped with neon-yellow tablemats. Below her table she could see the tops of the orange Day Lilies growing alongside the porch balustrade. A basket of coral pink Geraniums hung on the iron pipe railing of the porch steps. She had bought them for Mother's Day last year and prided herself on the offshoots growing in five pots setting at the edges of each front porch step.

Each day she sat at the glass topped table surrounded by flowers and warm sun. This was a sad time for Kathryn. She needed to cheer herself. Her summerhouse in the North Woods overlooked the local river running through her village. Absently she listened to the fast water splash over the rocks. Her heart was far away at her Midwestern farm home where she grew up amidst corn and hayfields,

Jacqueline K. Kelsey, Ph.D.

an apple orchard and a big flower and vegetable garden. A long winding road, like the river, led from the tall cement entrance gate to the farmhouse set among the Cedar trees on top of the hill.

Kathryn's mother and father lived at Gateway Farm with their family dog Gigi, a miniature Schnauzer. Gigi had come from Missouri to live with the family fourteen years ago when Zsa Zsa, the other much-loved Schnauzer, had died of a liver disease. Gentle Gigi had come to soothe their sad hearts with her puppy ways.

Gigi was an older dog now. Her black eyes had turned bluish; the vet had noticed she was losing her sight. Every afternoon she slept in her bed on the black and blue plaid round cushion, plopped down in a big leather chair setting near the door. The wooden ceiling fan whirred to keep her cool.

When Kathryn had returned home to the farm in May, Gigi slept for the whole afternoon almost every day. If anyone tried to pick Gigi up, she would growl, as if she were afraid of being hurt. It surprised Kathryn when she growled at her because they had always been close friends. In the past they would walk down to the woods on Stagecoach Road, past the old farm water tower, and over the hilly field into the woods. Gigi would sniff trails and lead the two of them to the far edge of the woods. But on their return, usually at the top of the field with the house in view, Kathryn would carry her friend the rest of the way home. Gigi always liked to see where she was going, so her four legs stuck out in front as she rode in the crook of Kathryn's arm.

In May, as usual, when they headed by the old barnwood garage, down the brick path to Stagecoach Road, Gigi skipped along almost dancing a Three-Legged Jig because she was going to the water tower. She looked back every few steps, like dogs do, to see if Kathryn was coming. As she skipped along, all of a sudden her legs folded under and she fell on her side. She was very still and whined. Kathryn feared Gigi was dying and talked to her gently, telling her that she would be okay while she stroked her head reassuringly. She wondered if she should leave to get her mother in case Gigi was dying, so that her mother could say good-bye. How could she do both? All of a sudden, Gigi's legs jerked and she came to. Like a mechanical toy, she stood up and wobbled on her unsure legs.

Kathryn and her mother took Gigi to the veterinarian several times to get the right dose of medication so that it would not be too strong for a little dog. The doctor could hear a slushing sound; her heart had a murmur just like Kathryn's mother. When Kathryn returned East to her summer home, she called frequently to get a report about Gigi. She realized there was nothing she could do so far away.

This week, when she had sunned at the table on the porch, she knew through her heart that her friend, Gigi, was dying. Over the phone she had heard Gigi barking at her father's car when he drove under the carport at noon. When he came home from the office, he was joyous because Gigi had just awakened. Ordinarily, her new medicine had completely sedated her for overnight and all morning. Kathryn's father reported on the phone that Gigi would not eat and just lay on her cushion in the big chair on the porch. He would never give her that strong medicine again, even if it kept her heart calm.

All week Kathryn knew the situation was getting worse as she sat at the table and looked out over the river. There was nothing to feel good about. The first day sitting on the porch she looked at the flowers. A hummingbird skirted above the flowers and sidled toward the railing near the table, not for long, not stopping to suck any nectar. The bird's iridescent green breast stood out brighter than any of Kathryn's flowers and she told it how beautiful it was.

The next day, Kathryn dug behind the house in the warm soil of the rock garden, terraced in the hillside at the bottom of the mountain. The hummingbird flew by her, up into the apple tree branches where she could see it easily. She was surprised to see it again, so close to her.

The third day, Kathryn thought about the bird as she

picked Hosta Lilies and tended the Rose trellis next to the garage. In the twinkle of an eye, the hummingbird joined her. It flew toward her, eye level, and flitted close by, not stopping to suck nectar but just seeming to be "in the neighborhood" of her and the Lilies.

On the fourth day, Kathryn stayed inside her house and sat at the dining room table where she could see out the windows looking toward the river. She would miss seeing the hummer. In the dining room, one small window looked beyond the kitchen toward the wood shed. Kathryn could see the Mother's Day Geranium pot hanging outside the kitchen window. Just as she was feeling sad about not seeing the hummingbird, she noticed movement above the Geranium pot. The hummingbird flew above it; she could see it after all!

No matter where Kathryn sat or worked, the bird was with her. She had a new companion! Her desire to see the bird grew. She was feeling happy to see it near her, to enjoy it flitting above the flowers, and to feel that it stayed a short while to give her joy. She always talked to it, telling the hummer how glad she was to see it, how wonderfully it moved. She had to smile excitedly as it flitted. There was a connection between the two because every time she thought of the hummingbird, it appeared almost immediately. As she became aware of the connection between her thoughts and its appearance, she was careful not to force a thought in order to see it arrive. Her desire seemed enough to bring the bird to her.

Two days went by until Kathryn left the inside of her house and returned to the porch. Knowing Gigi's death was near, another part of her, Kathryn's soul, lifted and she felt safe from despair. There was a peace or shelter like a harbor of relief. Had the hummingbird brought Kathryn enough relief that she was able to handle Gigi's death? The bird had not returned for two days and she wanted to will it into her presence, to be reassured that she could depend on the hummingbird for joy. She knew this was wrong to manipulate, to force what she wanted.

Sitting on the porch at her writing table, she reminded herself to desire, rather than to force, what she wanted. She looked toward the river, to the other side, and far in the distance she could see a dark object coming toward her with the speed of a dart. The forceful missile sped through the trees on the other side of the river, crossed over, and jettisoned through the birch limbs. So fast it flew! Kathryn could not see its colors, to be sure it were she. Across the road, over the picket fence, past the flower tops, and along the railing. She recognized her hummer and squealed softly, "You are so wonderful to be able to fly so fast; I wish you could stop!" The hummingbird turned the corner post at the far end of the porch. It was gone.

She was still thinking about how skillful the bird was and how beautifully it danced above the flowers. All of a sudden, within ten seconds, the hummer streaked by the corner post again, towards her. It had done a double-turn and was back, above the flowers right in front of her table. The bird danced in one place without taking a sip of nectar.

Jacqueline K. Kelsey, Ph.D.

In fact, Kathryn had never seen her sip nectar from any of the flowers. The hummingbird had always danced above the flowers. Kathryn was thrilled; she felt glee and joy. The hummingbird had brought her joy at the saddest moment of her life. The bird looked at Kathryn and beat her wings for as long as Kathryn needed to be convinced that she had been her companion all week—bringing her joy.

The hummingbird double-beat its way back around the post to who knows where. Past the kitchen window, over the wood shed roof, to the apple trees in the rock garden, up the hillside to the mountain or perhaps back to the garage border of Hosta Lilies and back over the river. The week was complete. Kathryn felt reassured that her friend cared about her feelings.

Yesterday had been the grand finale. Today it seemed like the visits were over. She sunned at the glass-topped table next to the porch balustrade. Looking over the tops of the flower stalks Kathryn noticed a new creature perched on the railing above the flowers—a crouching bumblebee.

It crouched very still. Kathryn wondered, "A bumblebee might go inside a trumpet flower and stay awhile?" She drew her head closer; carefully she put her face next to it and the bee remained still. She asked, "What is wrong?" The bee did not budge. Perhaps it was sick—missing a leg or wing? What could she do? She would take a petal from a flower and lay the petal next to the bee. When she carefully placed the bright pink Geranium petal next to it on the balustrade and the bee did not move, she knew something was wrong. She left to go into the house and sit at the dining room table for a short while, to be by herself. When she returned, the bee was gone. She looked everywhere for it. Had it fallen off the railing? It was nowhere—a mystery. There was no more thought, only Kathryn's wondering.

In September, when she returned to her Midwestern farm home, Kathryn's mother told her when Gigi had died. On that afternoon when the bumblebee lay close and let her put a petal next to it, their friend Gigi had died. When she told her mother about the bee, her mother quoted the verse "Death has no sting." Kathryn could see the motionless bee on the railing and believed the bee had been the messenger of death.

Kathryn went out to her mother's garden where Gigi was buried. A cement statue of a Schnauzer dog had been placed over the grave. A gift from Kathryn's sister, Anne, the life-size statue decorated the garden with life's image. It was difficult to imagine the real dog's body being dead, inert as the stone. Kathryn's mind could not put body and spirit together when the feeling of loss was so tender. While sitting on the white wrought iron garden bench she felt how dear life was.

Immediately, from out of nowhere, a hummingbird circled around her. It was there in the moment and then it was gone. Kathryn realized quickly that the spirit of Gigi danced above the flowers bringing her joy just as she had in their North Woods' garden. Gigi's spirit lived in the hummingbird.

Your story is sacred. View it as a parable for your on-going inspiration.

THE WILD CAT

"The cat was close enough for Kathryn to peer at its penny-size yellow eyes.... It looked like an owl."

There is a neighborhood myth that each spring a moose comes down the mountainside behind Kathryn and John's house onto the blacktop street along the river.

Wildlife loves Kathryn's neighborhood along the river. When Kathryn's parents from the Midwest visited on her birthday last fall, a raccoon sat in the Crabapple tree hanging over the porch roof. The raccoon stared down at her while she talked to it. The tall, old tree is a haven for birds, too. They sit and wait in turn to fly to the bird feeder nailed to the balustrade railing.

Kathryn's dead-end street alongside the river makes a turn-around difficult. Not many people drive down the street. Most of the traffic is carolers at Christmas, joggers in the spring, and fast walkers from the local businesses over their noon hours each day during the summer and fall.

On a summer morning in July, Kathryn backed out of the garage and turned toward the dead-end of the street to back up in the neighbor's drive. When she drove by her home, Kathryn noticed a black and tan striped tabby cat sitting in the middle of the top step **beneath the tall black door.** Kathryn had heard there was a wild cat on the hill behind their house.

"The cat took a liberty to sit on our porch," she mused. Several times she had seen it walking on the ridge behind the house, but it was too far away to talk to. In fact, John chased all cats away so she did not want to attract it. A week later, after seeing the tabby on top of the hill, she heard terrible cat screams coming from behind the house. She ran to the kitchen window where she could see the neighbor's gray Angora pin-wheeling down the hillside, near the big drainage pipe that carries hillside water to the river. The tabby cat and the gray Angora made a flying wheel down the hill as they fought. She could see blood on the gray cat's shoulder.

When Kathryn told the neighbors about their Angora cat, she learned that the striped cat was wild and she was warned that it could have rabies. Again, when Kathryn drove by her house to turn around at the neighbor's, she saw the tabby sitting on the top porch step. She looked like a pet, Kathryn speculated. Was it the same cat? Like a striped sphinx ruling over of the house, the wild creature sunned herself peacefully with closed eyes.

John did not want cats because of their bird feeder tray. When his father-in-law had come to visit, he had given them giant bags of seeds, one especially for wild birds, and a huge plastic trash can to put the seed in so it would stay dry. To keep animals out, like the raccoon, he had tied the lid down with a piece of rope. John and Kathryn also had attracted a new yard friend, a ground squirrel, who returned each year when they put out the birdseed.

The first year, John and Kathryn had named the ground squirrel Elizabeth. Kathryn remembered similar scamps from their family's vacation to the Colorado Rockies when she was a teenager. Kathryn's sister, Anne, wrote a children's story series about the adventures of one squirrel named "Timothy Timberline." Like the Colorado chipmunks, Elizabeth was friendly. Half the size of a gray squirrel, she sported a bushy, flicking tail. She looked dressed up with the black and white stripes on her back.

When John worked in the yard pulling weeds, Elizabeth sat on the nearby Cherry tree stump which was left after a windstorm. She chitted at John, as squirrels do, for fifteen minutes. Perhaps she was decoying John away from the entrance to her underground house near the roundel of flowers. The hole at the top of her tunnel was the size of a mustard jar lid.

Sometimes Kathryn would walk out to the roundel to pick flowers and would forget about Elizabeth's house entrance. Several times Elizabeth ran by underfoot, coming out or going in, so fast that Kathryn would stumble to prevent herself from stepping on her.

Some mornings Elizabeth chitted from the roof edge of the garden shed when Kathryn dug the flower garden along the back rock wall under the kitchen window.

Elizabeth puffed and chitted and Kathryn would say, "Good morning, Elizabeth. I'm so glad to see you. Aren't you cute with your sporty tail and striped back? You're good company for me."

During the second summer, knowing Elizabeth and the wild cat, John and Kathryn drove to the Midwest to see their families. On the way they took a vacation through the Hudson River Valley in New York. They were gone for three weeks; the grass in the side yard, in front of the woodshed, grew one and one-half feet high while they were away.

When they returned, John had to mow over each path several times. When he finally did mow the grass blades down to a two-inch height, the bleached grass and the formerly lush green yard looked anemic. In the late afternoon sun, when they walked the flower borders, Kathryn pointed to the high spots of ground; she paused. "No!" A pile of crawling insects, a handful of slugs? There were feet and legs. Were they lizards? They were too big. Kathryn could see they were so small they would not be able to live without their mother. Some of them lay limp. She felt scared and helpless. For the first time, Kathryn had no suggestion about what to do. She turned to John. John shook his head. He had disturbed their nest when he mowed. Some had been mangled by the electric mower blades. Kathryn covered her face.

She and John decided that the only kind thing was to move all of them to another area of grass. John lifted them in handfuls of grass to a mound across the road at the top of the riverbank. John felt sad that when they were trying to take care of nature and create beauty, something in nature had been destroyed.

Kathryn felt guilty. Perhaps they should have moved the creatures near the house. But there was no tall grass left. They should have gathered some and left them where the mother could find them. All Kathryn could think of was that they were too small to take care. The thought of the mother coming back for them did not occur to her in time. Perhaps her thought was that they were like birds whose mothers would not return when their nests were disturbed.

She and John had intruded in a wild area of the yard where the grass had been free. It was not a natural cycle of life and death for the new wild life. On the porch she and John talked about Elizabeth. Coming home from vacation was a letdown. John said, "I have not seen her by the roundel. She has not chitted from the Cherry stump."

Kathryn quietly spoke: "The creatures we found were her babies, I am sure." She thought Elizabeth had nested near the woodshed where the birdseed was kept in the garbage can. John had seen that Elizabeth had chewed a big hole in the garbage can lid so she could scamper in and out of the seed bag inside. They wondered if she would go away now. Kathryn whispered, "Nature seems so fragile—we destroyed it so easily. How unfortunate for the creatures. For Elizabeth. How disheartening for us."

* * *

After receiving Nancy's letter, Kathryn planned to

visit for one of three vacation weeks in Northern Maine on a fishing island where her friend lived. The trip planned in her mind. John could meet her at the ferry dock in Bar Harbor and they could drive north into Canada and take another ferry to Nova Scotia and Prince Edward Island.

The house was in order, the flowers had been watered and the grass mowed. All the mail had been read and the bills paid. They had recovered from the mowing incident by the woodshed in their routines of settling back home. They would be able to go north to Nova Scotia after Kathryn's visit to the fishing island, like Kathryn dreamed.

During the week's visit on the fishing island, Nancy echoed Kathryn's idea. Kathryn and John could meet her at the ferry dock after the mail boat pulled in and the two could drive north toward Nova Scotia. It rained all week; the girls quilted indoors and walked to the island café for steaming chowder. Kathryn visited the island library and discovered on the third floor a commemorative poem to the 1600's settlers of the bay area. She connected with her 1600's ancestors from a nearby island.

The old dock timbers creaked as John and Kathryn walked away from the mail boat. Nearing the car, John gave over to the notion of new adventure; he had missed out on the girls' week at the fishing village. Kathryn mulled over her own dream and Nancy's suggestion to go north.

During the afternoon, Kathryn and John drove inland a few miles to take pictures of nearby genealogical sites—Kathryn's 13th generation ancestors, the cove where George Felt owned land, the road leading to the bay, the falls, and the cemetery. At one time he had been credited the honor of settling the whole area. They made plans to return after their trip north to attend a historical society lecture and to look at books of deeds in the library. After buying bread at the village bakery and buying an early land division map at the town clerk's office they headed farther north into Maine.

Kathryn had heard about the rock-bound coast of

Jacqueline K. Kelsey, Ph.D.

Maine from her mother-in-law who always wanted to see it. Just before they left on their trip, Kathryn had received a call from her parents in the Midwest with the disturbing news of her father-in-law's passing. Her mother-in-law was blind in old age. Kathryn would have to be the eyes for her to see the ocean coast.

The first evening in a coastal village, where they ate a seafood supper, the waitress suggested a side trip for them on the new Catamaran fast ferry to Nova Scotia. A dream come true. Kathryn would make this trip for her mother, too, who had read Longfellow's "Evangeline" to her high school English classes when she taught. Kathryn remembered her mother baking a red cake from a family recipe in the Louisiana Cajun region to which Evangeline's countrymen fled.

This vacation was becoming a fairy tale trip topped off by a Sunday morning ride on a four-mast schooner when they returned to Bar Harbor. John relaxed in the warm, still air. Rarely did Kathryn see him so at ease.

Their captain had said, "The wind takes the boat where it will!" They sailed around the islands which they had viewed from their mountain-top drive two weeks before.

After camping in Nova Scotia the long drive back from Bar Harbor to their home in the North Woods seemed short. They decided to camp an extra night so they could research genealogy and enjoy bay area scenery on the daytime drive home. Maybe Kathryn would see a moose. She always hoped to see one on her street at home.

They were glad to return to their woodsy home along the Moose River. The sunset mountain glared pink in the early evening sky. Instead of unpacking the car, they wanted to go into the house together after being gone a week. Home on the river seemed like a Never-Neverland retreat. And truly they had been gone all summer with their visit to family in the Midwest and the trip through the Hudson River Valley.

Coming through **the tall black door,** they paused to see the flowers and trees and to hear the river. They drank it in. Kathryn admired the Delphinium towering over the balustrade. Her attention was drawn to the bottom of the porch rail by the brightness of the neon pink Geraniums beaming through the gingerbread carving. Beneath the balustrade she noticed a strange-looking tube on the blue runner carpet. She bent closer to see and touch the sausage.

Kathryn picked it up and felt the skin; horrified she called to John. It was the innards of an animal. She knew. It was too big to be a mouse. "Oh, no!" she moaned. When she dropped it back to the carpet they both realized what it was. John picked it up and tossed it. There was no body or spirit. He was tossing remains and getting it away from Kathryn; he was angry.

Kathryn told John they should have buried the remains with the other dead creatures. He asked "How could the wild cat time his conquest with our return even before he saw us?" It was the nature of the beast to kill and display its bounty. On the family farm in Illinois, Kathryn's cat, Oscar, would wake her in the night with a strange cry from under her bedroom window near the porch door. Sometimes it was a mouse or a bird. Was the wild cat welcoming them home? Ahead of time or on time? How uncanny; a wild futurist.

Nature's full circle. They sat on the top porch step. John and Kathryn recalled the mowing tragedy when they had cared for the grass and beautified the yard. Survival – generation after generation. Building homes, surviving, dying, establishing kingdoms, protecting them.

In the late fall, the wild cat strolled through the front yard across the road. It had moved down from the ridge. From her Adirondack chair in the side yard Kathryn watched it cross in the front of the dying tree that hosted a woodpecker. The cat was close enough for Kathryn to see its penny size yellow eyes and the gray fur tufts sticking out its ears. It looked like an owl. She sat musing: were she and John a new generation becoming eyes for the previous one—her mother and mother-in-law?

Jacqueline K. Kelsey, Ph.D.

This Spring Kathryn and John adopted a new ground squirrel they call "Buster Brown." He races up and down the Crabapple tree where the raccoon stared down at Kathryn last fall. Elizabeth's tunnel near the Cherry tree stump is the right size for him, too. The ground entrance hole is still the size of a mustard jar lid.

Imagination becomes the ability to envision. It is faith.

THE DANCING RABBIT

"...Kathryn held the rabbit close to her. John called to her as he went out the tall black door: 'You cannot hold the rabbit forever.'"

Jacqueline K. Kelsey, Ph.D.

About four o'clock, Kathryn walked down River Street toward the village. As she passed in front of her old gray garage, she turned to check John's painting on the garage doors. To her surprise, at the bottom of the first door huddled a clean, tan and white rabbit with long ears. She had not seen any neighborhood rabbits before. At a safe distance she froze like the rabbit and watched.

Feeling safe, the rabbit unfroze and hopped back and forth along the bottom of the two framed garage doors. It had found a sanctuary in its path, hopping back and forth. "It looks so small," she thought. "Oh, how alone. The rabbit must belong to someone," she announced to the trees along the river.

Yesterday in the bookstore, while she was waiting to pay, Kathryn had found a book on the shelf beneath the cashier's counter entitled *The Fiddler of the Northern Lights* by Natalie Kinsey-Warnock. The young boy in the story was carrying carrots in his pocket with the hope of seeing rabbits dance. Earlier in the day, while interviewing for a job, a nun had asked Kathryn, who was a storyteller, "Where is God in the story of your life?" Kathryn wondered about her life's work as a storyteller and whether or not it helped others to lead more meaningful lives. Seeing this real rabbit today was an unusual event after finding the book yesterday and being asked the question about God in her life. She was curious about the meaning of the serendipity.

As she stood and watched the brown and white rabbit, Kathryn thought of her partner, John, who had been painting the doors the day before while she was at the book store. Like the rabbit, he must have felt alone. Painting was difficult for him because he had wanted to do a good job. Because he had not stirred the primer, he had painted the big doors with just the oil from the top of the can. Today he was going to need to paint the first coat again. Perhaps the rabbit was teaching him and her about courage to restore the old house?

Kathryn could not leave the rabbit and continue her walk to the village. Maybe a big dog would come along; the rabbit's life would be jeopardized. Kathryn saw that her neighbor's car was gone and she thought, "Oh no, Nancy cannot help me." Kathryn was afraid to pick up the rabbit because it might bite her—the other neighbor's cat had bitten her earlier that fall. She stood and watched the rabbit for a few minutes and decided to get help from the neighborhood.

Like their garage, the old yellow house across the street needed painting too. Old boards hung loose along the foundation and the window screens had baseball-size holes in them. Tenants had moved in and out. Kathryn was afraid to go to the drab yellow house and decided to check out the other neighbor who lived in the small green house beyond it.

The man in the green house had been friendly when he walked by and said "hello" the day before while John painted the garage doors and she painted the fence. She knocked at the door and waited. Instead of the friendly man, a young teenager answered and told her that the rabbit belonged to Steven, who lived in the big, old, yellow house. Kathryn was thrilled to find the rabbit's owner.

She hurried back home to see if the rabbit were okay. At the same time, her friend Nancy drove up in a van. Nancy almost skipped over to see the surprise when Kathryn waved both hands to her. Her friend was not afraid to pick up the rabbit because she had raised goats and chickens and she loved animals. Nancy held the rabbit close. "It's cold," she said. Kathryn held the rabbit, too.

Thinking they could put it in a cage, Kathryn asked Nancy if she had a dog carrier. Soon Nancy came back with a huge dog carrier for her Rottweiler. She took the rabbit from Kathryn and set him inside the front corner, near the wire door. In the meantime, Kathryn had run home to get some old towels to make a soft bed in the carrier. John had brought the towels as a gift from Holland several years ago. She did not care about them anymore; in fact, she had wanted a good use for them.

The girls brought the cage with the rabbit sitting on the towels through the gate, up the porch steps, through **the tall black door** into Kathryn's living room. Early in the morning, Kathryn had built a fire in the wood stove. When they set the dog carrier on the soft carpet they could see the little rabbit cozily nestled into the towels in the back corner of the big cage. Kathryn went to the refrigerator to get some lettuce. Nancy gave him one leaf and he nibbled it right up. Kathryn gave him another leaf and he stuffed it in with a wiggle of his nose.

Kathryn and Nancy decided to surprise John and leave the cage in the living room. They put an international newspaper on the top of the cage to cover Nancy's name and left quickly, hoping to surprise John when he came home. After walking with Nancy to her house, Kathryn went on to the village.

When Kathryn walked home from the village she heard the rattling, black pickup drive up in front of the yellow house. "Oh! Somebody from the yellow house.

Jacqueline K. Kelsey, Ph.D.

I will be friendly," Kathryn thought as she went up to the man and his wife in the truck. When he opened the door to get out she could see his muddy boots. His flannel shirt cuffs and wrists stuck together with caked mud. His dark eyebrows hung over his deep-set eyes. Kathryn wondered if he worked in the woods.

    The man had said "hello" earlier in the week when she was painting the fence, so he recognized her. She told him about the rabbit—how the rabbit was sitting on pink and white striped towels in the dog cage set in front of the woodstove in the living room.

    He smiled a little and Kathryn could see that he felt good about the rabbit. He looked rough. The girl-like woman said she knew Steven was visiting and would be back soon. She would tell him where the rabbit was. Kathryn wondered how they knew where Steven was. How did they know the boy?

    At the end of the day, John came up the porch steps through **the tall black door** into the living room and saw the cage on the carpet, but he did not pay much attention; in fact, he did not want to look inside because he was afraid it was a dog! He did not want a pet.

Kathryn had to take John by the hand to show him what was in the cage. John watched while she pulled the rabbit from the back of the cage and cuddled it close to her. She passed the rabbit to him and he, too, held the rabbit. "This is a very special rabbit," she told John. In the meantime, Kathryn had put the rabbit storybook, which she read yesterday, on top of the cage. (She had folded John's international newspaper and put it next to the firewood.)

The two sat by the fire while Kathryn read the story aloud. John and Kathryn noted that, indeed, this was the "hopeful" rabbit of the story. John began to hold the rabbit closely. Kathryn wondered if he felt less alone. She certainly did! When he went out to re-paint the doors on the garage, he called to her, "You cannot hold the rabbit forever." She put it up to her neck and held it like a baby.

Trying to warm it because its ears were still cold,

she wondered if its furry body were still cold. Instead, she felt its warm body and tried to absorb all the heat of the rabbit into her chest and into her heart. Kathryn thought she could hold it all day, maybe all night, but decided to return it to the cage.

She went out to help John paint the rest of the garage door and the fence. The fence was a soft sky blue. It looked beautiful and all the neighbors had been admiring it. Kathryn was finishing the fence gate that John had primed on the front and the back. He was painting a second white coat on the garage door where the rabbit had hopped back and forth before she and Nancy had rescued it.

While Kathryn painted the last board on the gate she felt someone near and turned around quickly to hear an announcement from a short boy with dark blonde hair. "I have come for my rabbit." Excitedly, Kathryn said, "Oh! You must be Steven!" Steven looked about ten. He was tall. She noticed his sandy hair, the same color as the rabbit's tan spots. "Your rabbit will be glad to see you. I found it this afternoon near the garage door about four o'clock."

"This morning when I came out to feed the rabbit, it was gone," he said. The girl-like woman in the black truck had told Kathryn the same thing. Now she realized that Steven was the son of the man and woman in the truck. With concern, Kathryn pointed out to Steven that the rabbit must have been out all morning. "Maybe it was out all night! It must have been very cold," she said. Steven explained that the rabbit did live outdoors and he was going to have to do something about the cage. He would bring in the rabbit this winter.

Kathryn and Steven walked along their picket fence, through the gate, and up the steps to **the tall black door**. It was time to return the rabbit. Inside the house, embers glowed in the wood stove. Nancy's dog cage set on the rose-pink rug; inside, the rabbit snuggled in the pink striped towels John had brought from Holland, and Steven and Kathryn sat on the floor next to the cage in front of the wood stove.

When Steven opened the cage, he could not reach the rabbit because it was in the corner. Kathryn offered to stretch for it but she saw that he could do it. He had to pull on the rabbit gently. The rabbit's head nuzzled under the corner of his shirt. Steven said, "See." He repeatedly pulled the corner of his shirt over the rabbit's paws to coax it. Soon the rabbit crawled up on his knee and snuggled into the crook of his leg.

Steven and Kathryn began to talk quietly while he snuggled the rabbit. She told him the story she had read to John about the fiddler and finding dancing rabbits. When she was finished, he began to tell her his story about the fiddler. "Oh yes, I know that one!" he said. "And the people began to dance and they danced together and soon everyone danced." He moved his arms and swayed his upper body. He loved the idea of dancing. Kathryn reminded Steven that the Grandpa in the story said he had told the story, over and over, about there being a fiddler who caused the Northern Lights to dance, even when he did not believe it, and, finally, it came true.

The Dance is what the boy, Steven, was so jubilant about. Kathryn asked Steven about his rabbit's name. "He doesn't have a name," he said. "I've never given him one." He pulled on his tan hair. "I just could not think of one." "I've got it!" exclaimed the boy. "Tappy!" And then he clicked his feet together, "Tappy Toes.'" Kathryn laughed as she watched him dance. "Did you say, 'Tappy Toes'?" Steven giggled. "Yes. 'Tappy' for short." And so "Tappy Toes" is what Steven named his rabbit. He had been going to take a picture of his rabbit and him together and go to the library to make lost rabbit signs at the end of the day. "I will bring you a picture of 'Tappy' and me tomorrow after school," Steven re-assured Kathryn.

Looking forward to seeing Steven again, Kathryn knew that the rabbit had danced for him when he held onto the hope of finding his rabbit. From reading the story,

Jacqueline K. Kelsey, Ph.D.

she had believed in finding rabbits when she discovered the rabbit in front of their garage doors. Because she was part of finding "Tappy Toes" Kathryn had grown in her desire to tell stories. She had found the answer to the nun's question whether or not God was in her life and stories. Because of "Tappy Toes" Kathryn would create new stories out of every-day miracles.

A childlike imagination is our transport to truth; we enable ourselves to manifest life's miracles everyday.

BACKWARDS AND FORWARDS

Kathryn felt free to give her china cupboard moose to the neighbor at the end of the street when he moved out West. She felt it was a genuine memento from River Street. His child had been a listener to the stories when they were told on River Street.

Several years later, on Kathryn's birthday, she wanted to celebrate by driving north to a nearby larger town where there were coffee shops and boutiques. As her car climbed the mountain incline on the sunny fall day, she noticed a large animal lying in the meridian. Pulling over, it was clear that a gentle moose cow had been hit and lay Immobile. When Kathryn got out of the car to walk closer, the moose and she looked long into each other's eyes. Her head was upright but she could not move even though she slightly agitated when Kathryn came toward her.

Kathryn saw peace and strength in her eyes. Backing away, Kathryn felt concern over agitating her when she could not get up. It seemed she had been hit in the back and legs.

Another car had stopped and the driver said he had phoned the state police. Death and birth sharing the same day of celebration tapped both of their strength and courage; life and death within a few minutes of experience. Moving on from life to death in the rear view mirror and back to life on the road north. Although this was not the gift Kathryn hope to give herself, the peace she received from the moose cow's eyes was like the looks she shared with a deer recently when one remained behind the herd which fled into the woods. It inquired about the humanity in its wild kingdom of the field. They looked at each other for as long as they needed to know that life prevails and renews in all forms, wild and human.

There is reassurance that Spring will always come.

A FINAL NOTE

On October 1, 2010 The gold house behind the gold picket fence succombed to a mudslide from the road bed above her. The mud surrounded her and filled the basement; she moved off her foundation. Walls cracked and torked. The chimney behind the woodstove toppled and the the old library wall caved under the force of the fallen tree.

"Housie," a pet name for the historic home on the national register, had to give way to the strong forces of rain and mountain -side terrain. Generation upon generation create new life as in the story "TheWild Cat." The home's two-story antique barn fell two years ago when the three old Red Oaks gave way on the hillside crushing the storybook barn of the "Dancing Rabbit" story.

Several years ago the hillside slid because of inadequate drainage. The two story house slid off of its foundation, only to be lifted and put back on a new basement.

Destiny is mysterious and present.

PEOPLE OF RIVER STREET

We remember our neighbors who go through the seasons together:

They admire the Crabapple tree when it is unusually creative, as it was the season these stories were written; several neighbors took pictures of the old, taller-than-the-house tree.

They notice the flowers along the picket fence as they come on. Some neighbors look for new blooms of Black-eyed Susans and Bleeding Hearts.

The children and caregivers gather at the oldest residents' home on the corner to hear the stories as they are written.

Hillside creatures join our lives along the river—the Orioles and Grey Heron, the deer on the steep hillside, a ground hog and her eight babies, and occasional bears.

Generations of village families have gathered on the front porch for family reunions. Young people have ice skated on the frozen river when it was dammed for the mill.

The village walked through **the tall black door** to use the village's early library housed on shelves at the far end of the living room where the wood stove burns.

And, always, we look for the Springtime moose who returns to River Street.

CREATE YOUR PARABLES

A. Create Seven To-Do Lists

Goal: Perceive God teaching you spiritual truths from the scriptures, through serendipitous life events with people and animals in nature.

#1 Motivate yourself to experience life beautifully by enjoying and creating beautiful places--natural and man-made ones.

Support: Each month, write the date on which you observe your life events.

_____ _____ _____

_____ _____ _____

_____ _____ _____

_____ _____ _____

IDENTIFY each month:

#2 Put yourself in situations because you feel it is appropriate based on current clues rather than on logic or assessment.

_____ _____ _____

_____ _____ _____

_____ _____ _____

_____ _____ _____

#3 Give up expectations others have of you to live a traditional work, life, and home style.

_____ _____ _____

_____ _____ _____

_____ _____ _____

_____ _____ _____

#4 Spend time with family and friends, pets and plants, the sky above and the ocean floor below--the tangible substances of God.

_____   _____   _____

_____   _____   _____

_____   _____   _____

_____   _____   _____

#5 Write and speak about your life events; help others to do the same by telling them what you do.

_____   _____   _____

_____   _____   _____

_____   _____   _____

_____   _____   _____

#6 Remind yourself that you are wealthy by Infinite plan and open yourself to express the plan.

_____ _____ _____

_____ _____ _____

_____ _____ _____

_____ _____ _____

#7 Live abundantly to experience that all of your needs are met.

_____ _____ _____

_____ _____ _____

_____ _____ _____

_____ _____ _____

B. Memorialize

Memorialize seven significant nature experiences. Write a brief account of each one and record the date of your entry.

Date _____

Date _____

Date _____

Date _____

Date _____

Date _____

Date _____

Live Your Life as Parable

Part 1:

What can you do to believe and do to live in parable?

Life Experience

1. Use life experience as the laboratory for learning to perceive whole relationships.

New Events

2. Pay attention quickly and closely to newness in events, surroundings, and people's actions.

Spiritual Truth

3. Perceive the spiritual truth in events.

Connected relationships

4. Accept the realities of time being circular, parallel, looped; therefore, the past and present, and future are one. Space is unlimited and contiguous.

Part II:

How do you know when you're living in parable?

The parable grows out of the reality of event. It comes from an imperative or unsure situation. It appears unplanned, unstructured or not imposed.

1. **What Happens**

   - You ask a question or make a request.

   - You see an unusual demonstration which connects with your life, although its significance may not be clear at the time.

2. **Characteristics of the Event**

   - It seems appropriate even though unusual.

   - There is close timing with other people or events in the past and present.

   - You have inner knowing that the event is significant.

   - The event seems complete as is.

- A sequel may follow. Events probably are part of a series over time.

3. **Characters in the parable**

    - The story includes a witness to see or tell the parable to; the other person (or animal or inanimate object or place in nature) sees the truth, also, which you believe.

    - There are other participants in the event:

        o Someone may serve you as an interpreter after the story.

        o During the story someone may join you as a guide.

        o You may meet a challenger or experience challenges to test the validity of your experience.

            ▪ The challenger will confirm the validity for you.
            ▪ You do not have to prove your experience.

Others with Sacred Story
A Parable Serves You and Others

It creates a spiritual truth from the mundane or common place.

- It seems larger than oneself.

- A sense of self is expanded.

- It reflects Eternal Truth.

- It feels alive with the Spirit of God.

It becomes "sacred story" because it is "your soul's response to nature."

Nature is God's creative expression –

You are one with God!

Sacred story is your soul's openness to God's demonstration of love.

Brainstorm and briefly name three experiences with sacred story.

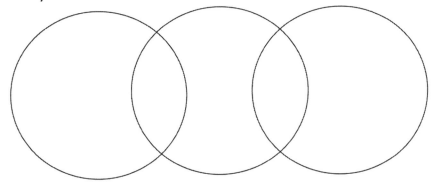

Show how the above experiences connect.

From the experiences above show how they are connected with arrows (for example, before and after, location, significance, characters, seasons, etc.).

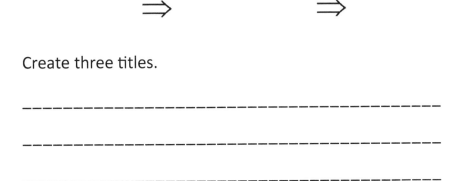

Create three titles.

_____

_____

_____

THE AUTHOR'S LIFE WORK

Dr. Kelsey is a master student, teacher, and performer of life stories, as well as an author of nature stories for children and adults. In addition to writing, traveling and working in the Northwest, Northeast, and South Pacific, she also tended the family's water tower cottage on their Midwestern pioneer farm and her own Apple Shed, an *atelier*, or "artists' cave," and created her own performing center.

In workshops across the nation she teaches from her book, *DANCING UP THE MOUNTAIN—a Story Notebook for Writing Your Own Life Stories*. Her sensitive guidance focuses on discovering the treasures in relationships, celebrations, work and everyday lives. She helps illuminate the uniqueness of our lives.

Inspiration for reaching our creative potential comes from "Creativity Circles" which she leads in the "atelier" at the APPLE SHED. Recorded stories and local radio programming on Sunday mornings support the community in the miracle of living serendipitously.

You may contact the author with your responses to the stories. For continuing inspiration, please order other books and c.d.'s from the author through her e-mail:

APPLESHED70@gmail.com

OTHER WORKS
Dancing Up the Mountain: a Guide
to Writing Your Life Stories

Listen in the Moment to Timeless Folks, c.d.

Dance Above the Flowers, c.d. (summer)

The Wild Cat and Miracle Moose, c.d. (fall and spring)
"May I Come In?" said the Sparrow, c.d. (winter)

Coming in 2011
Flying from the Mountain Top:
a fireside reader to inspire
Going the Distances